# UNBEL
# BASKETBALL
# LEGENDS

## STORIES FOR KIDS

**DREAM BIGGER BOOKS**

# TABLE OF CONTENTS

# INTRODUCTION
## Welcome young readers!

Basketball is more than just a sport; it's a rich tapestry of history, drama, and unforgettable moments that have captivated fans for generations. This book, "Unbelievable Basketball Stories," takes you on a journey through some of the most iconic and awe-inspiring events in basketball history. From record-breaking achievements to dramatic comebacks and legendary performances, each chapter brings to life the passion and excitement that define America's pastime. Whether you're a lifelong fan or new to the game, these stories showcase the resilience, determination, and sheer magic that make basketball an enduring part of our culture. Join us as we celebrate the heroes, the unforgettable moments, and the enduring spirit of basketball that continues to inspire and unite fans around the world.

# CHAPTER 1
## Michael Jordan - The Last Shot

It was 1998, Game 6 of the NBA Finals, and the Chicago Bulls were locked in a fierce battle against the Utah Jazz. With just seconds left on the clock, the Bulls found themselves down by one point. The energy in the arena was electric; every fan was on their feet, their eyes glued to the court. This was no ordinary game.

For Michael Jordan, this could be the final act of an illustrious career, one that had already been filled with six championships, five MVP awards, and countless unforgettable moments. But one last shot could close the chapter on his career in the most perfect way possible.

Jordan, the undisputed superstar of the Bulls, had faced pressure before, but this moment was different. A sixth title was on the line, and the ball was in his hands. With just a few seconds remaining, Jordan stood at the top of the key, staring down the basket, fully aware of the significance of the moment. He had trained for this his entire life, had taken this shot countless times in practice, but now, under the spotlight, it all came down to this. The world was watching, and the weight of history rested on his shoulders.

In the final 9.6 seconds of the game, Jordan took control. He dribbled to his right, locking eyes with his defender, Bryon Russell, a 6'6", 216-pound athlete who had been tasked with guarding Jordan throughout the game. But Jordan was no ordinary player; he was a master, a creator of opportunities even in the tightest situations. As he drove to his right, he suddenly crossed over to his left, causing Russell to stumble just enough for Jordan to find the space he needed.

In a flash, Jordan launched himself into the air. His shoulders hunched, head down, eyes fixed on the basket, he released the ball. The arena fell into a deafening silence as the ball arced through the air. It was a shot Jordan had practiced a thousand times, but never had so much rested on a single moment. If it went in, it would do more than win the game; it would forever cement his legacy as the greatest of all time.

That was the moment, the pinnacle of Michael Jordan's career, a career defined by greatness and the pursuit of perfection. For Jordan, it was the culmination of a journey filled with obstacles and adversity—from the physical toll of injuries to the fierce competition of the NBA, and even his own battles with self-doubt. Yet, no matter the challenge, Jordan always found a way to rise above it. His unmatched work ethic, focus, and ability to perform under the most intense pressure set him apart from the rest.

Jordan's "Last Shot" is not merely a highlight in the annals of sports history; it is a testament to tenacity, hard work, and the unyielding desire to be the best. It serves as a reminder that true success isn't just about natural talent; it's about dedication, resilience, and the courage to seize the moment when it matters most. Michael Jordan's legacy continues to inspire athletes and fans alike, showing that with relentless effort and a refusal to give up, anything is possible. The "Last Shot" is more than just a game-winning moment—it is the embodiment of Michael Jordan's legacy and the enduring spirit of basketball.

# Fun facts

1) Baseball Break: Jordan left basketball in 1993 to play baseball before returning in 1995.

2) Jumpman: The "Jumpman" logo is based on Jordan's famous dunking pose.

3) Flu Game: Jordan scored 38 points in the 1997 Finals despite having the flu.

# Trivia

**How many NBA championships did Michael Jordan win with the Chicago Bulls?**

a) 4

b) 5

c) 6

# CHAPTER 2
## Kobe Bryant - The 81-Point Game

On January 22, 2006, Kobe Bryant authored one of the greatest performances in basketball history. Kobe's Los Angeles Lakers were facing the Toronto Raptors, and early on, it seemed like just another regular-season game. However, by the time the final buzzer sounded, Kobe had scored 81 points, a feat that trails only Wilt Chamberlain's 100-point game in 1962 as the second-highest total in NBA history.

Kobe was unstoppable that night. From the outset, he was in the zone, and every shot he took, whether from the three-point line, mid-range, or in the paint, seemed destined to find the bottom of the net. His teammates and opponents alike could see that Kobe was not just playing a game—he was on a mission. His focus was singular: to win. And he was prepared to do whatever it took to achieve that.

With each passing second and every basket, it became clear that this wasn't just a hot streak—it was something much more special. The Raptors had no answer for Kobe. He drained three-pointers, drove relentlessly to the hoop, and calmly sank his free throws. But what stood out most was Kobe's mental toughness. When the Lakers fell behind in the first half, Kobe didn't back down. Instead, he pushed even harder, determined to lead his team to victory.

By the third quarter, Kobe had already scored more points than most players would in an entire game. The crowd at LA's Staples Center was on its feet, fully aware that they were witnessing history. Each basket was met with louder cheers, the scoreboard ticking ever higher as disbelief spread through the arena. But this wasn't just about points—it was about willpower, about refusing to be denied, about leading by example in the most extraordinary way.

Kobe's intensity didn't wane in the fourth quarter. His teammates kept feeding him the ball because they knew they were part of something extraordinary. The Raptors tried everything—double-teams, getting right up in his face—yet nothing worked. Kobe was locked in, and there was no stopping him. When the game finally ended, Kobe had scored 81 points, leading the Lakers to a 122-104 victory.

That 81-point game wasn't just about scoring; it was about work ethic, about mental toughness, about striving for perfection. As Kobe himself said: "I have no desire to break that record. My desire is to break the idea of what's possible, to inspire kids to dream, to be inspired, and to use whatever resources they have to achieve the impossible." And indeed, Kobe did just that.

Kobe's 81-point game made waves through the sporting community. It was seen as a testament to what one can achieve into your dream, a reminder of what it means to commit. For young players, it was a lesson on what it means to 'go hard'. Kobe's historic night showed that greatness is about so much more than talent. It's about depths of will and desire to go beyond what you're capable of, to continue when everyone says you can't.

The 81-point game is surely one of the most memorable performances in sports history. It's a perfect illustration of what happens when preparedness meets opportunity. For Kobe, it was just another day at the office, another game when the Mamba Mentality took over and pushed him to do something great. He became known as one of the best scorers of all time, and this performance will live on in basketball history as an inspiration for future players.

# Fun facts

1) Kobe's Record: Kobe's 81 points are the most scored by a single player in the modern NBA era.

2) Second-Highest: His 81-point game is second only to Wilt Chamberlain's 100-point game in 1962.

3) Single Quarter: Kobe scored 28 of his 81 points in the third quarter alone.

# Trivia

**Against which team did Kobe Bryant score his 81 points?**

A) Miami Heat

B) Toronto Raptors

C) Boston Celtics

# CHAPTER 3
## LeBron James - The Chosen One

LeBron James was dubbed "The Chosen One" from virtually the moment he emerged on the basketball scene. Raised in Akron, Ohio, LeBron was a basketball prodigy during his elementary school years. By the time he reached high school, he was a national sensation. His combination of skill, athleticism, and basketball intelligence was far beyond his peers.

The pressure was immense and relentless. LeBron wasn't just expected to make it to the NBA—he was expected to dominate the league and live up to comparisons with Michael Jordan and Magic Johnson. As a high schooler, LeBron's games were broadcast nationally, and the media frenzy surrounding him was unprecedented. Yet, through it all, LeBron kept his composure. He thrived under pressure, determined not only to meet the expectations but to exceed them.

Drafted by the Cleveland Cavaliers as the top pick of the 2003 NBA Draft, LeBron entered the league as a 19-year-old phenom. It didn't take long for the world to see that he was special. In his rookie year, LeBron averaged over 20 points per game and earned the NBA Rookie of the Year award. The kid from Akron had officially arrived as one of the league's brightest stars, but this was only the beginning.

Within a few years, LeBron became known for his versatility. Standing 6'9" and weighing 250 pounds, he had the body of a power forward, but he passed with the vision and skill of a point guard. He could score, rebound, assist, and defend at an elite level. His rare combination of size, speed, and basketball IQ made him nearly impossible to guard. As his game evolved, LeBron led his teams deep into the playoffs year after year. However, despite his incredible performances, he came up short of his ultimate goal: winning an NBA championship.

In 2010, LeBron made one of the most controversial decisions in NBA history. After seven years with the Cleveland Cavaliers, he announced his departure from the team in a primetime special on ESPN, titled "The Decision." LeBron revealed that he would be joining the Miami Heat, forming a superteam with Dwyane Wade and Chris Bosh. The announcement shocked the sports world, and many fans, especially in Cleveland, felt betrayed by his departure.

However, the move paid off. LeBron earned his first NBA title in 2012 with the Miami Heat and added another championship in 2013. He had finally conquered basketball's ultimate stage, shedding the narrative that he couldn't deliver in big moments. Yet, even after reaching the pinnacle of success in Miami, LeBron felt that his journey wasn't complete—he had unfinished business back in Cleveland.

LeBron rejoined the Cleveland Cavaliers in 2014, driven by a singular mission: to bring a championship to his home state of Ohio. Two years later, in 2016, LeBron led the Cavaliers to an improbable victory in the NBA Finals. Facing the Golden State Warriors, a team that had set the record for most wins in a regular season, the Cavaliers found themselves in a 3-1 deficit in the series—an almost insurmountable challenge. However, LeBron led the Cavaliers to three consecutive wins, defeating the Warriors and delivering Cleveland its first-ever NBA championship.

From "The Chosen One" to a four-time NBA champion, LeBron's journey is a testament to his perseverance and dedication. His legendary performances on the court are matched by his efforts off the court, where he has emerged as a leader in social justice, education, and community empowerment. LeBron James's legacy is not just about basketball—it's about rising to the highest expectations and using his platform to create positive change in the world.

# Fun facts

1) Rookie of the Year: LeBron won NBA Rookie of the Year in 2004 after averaging 20.9 points per game in his debut season.

2) Triple-Threat: LeBron is one of only a few players in NBA history to record over 30,000 points, 10,000 rebounds, and 10,000 assists.

3) Akron's School: In 2018, LeBron opened the I PROMISE School in Akron, Ohio, for at-risk children, providing free education and support.

# Trivia

**How many NBA championships has LeBron James won?**

A) 2
B) 3
C) 4

# CHAPTER 4

## Larry Bird vs. Magic Johnson - Rivalry and Respect

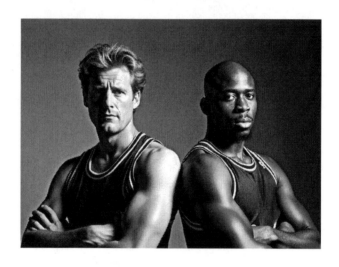

The rivalry between Larry Bird and Magic Johnson is the stuff of basketball legend. It began with their first meeting in the 1979 NCAA Championship Game. Bird's Indiana State Sycamores faced Magic's Michigan State Spartans, and came up short: Magic's Spartans won the national title. But that game was only the beginning of a rivalry that would come to define the 1980s in the NBA.

Bird and Magic entered the league that same year, both playing for storied franchises—Bird for the Boston Celtics, and Magic for the Los Angeles Lakers.

These two players were unlike any others from the moment they stepped onto an NBA court. Larry Bird, with his astonishing shooting range, basketball IQ, and relentless grittiness, epitomized the hard-nosed spirit of Boston basketball. Magic Johnson, with his dazzling passing, showmanship, and charismatic leadership, brought the flashy, up-tempo style of Los Angeles to life. Their rivalry came to symbolize the "coastal wars"—the blue-collar toughness of Bird's Boston Celtics against the Hollywood glitz of Magic's Lakers.

For most of the 1980s, Bird and Magic took turns leading their teams to multiple NBA championships, often squaring off in the Finals. Between 1980 and 1989, the Lakers and Celtics combined to win eight of 10 NBA titles, with Bird and Magic facing off in three Finals series. Each time they matched up, it was a battle of titans, with the stakes higher than ever. These games weren't just about winning a championship; they were about personal pride and the desire to prove who was the best.

Even in the midst of their fierce competition, Bird and Magic always maintained a deep respect for each other. They understood that to be considered the greatest, each had to defeat the other. Their games weren't just tests of skill —they were tests of will, with both players pushing each other to their limits. Behind the scenes, despite the heated battles on the court, their mutual respect began to build a foundation for something even greater.

The rivalry reached its peak during the 1984 NBA Finals, when the Celtics and Lakers faced off in an unforgettable seven-game series. The games were physical, emotional, and intense, with Bird and Magic at the heart of the action. The Celtics ultimately won, giving Bird a long-sought victory over his rival. But Magic had his revenge the following year in 1985, when the Lakers defeated the Celtics in the Finals, becoming the first team to beat Boston in a championship series.

While they fiercely competed for championships throughout the 1980s, by the late 1980s, Bird and Magic's relationship had evolved from rivals to friends. The turning point in their friendship came in 1991 when Magic was diagnosed as HIV positive, leading to his immediate retirement from the NBA. Bird was one of the first to offer public support, standing by his old rival in a time of need. Their friendship only grew from there, and when Magic returned to play in the 1992 NBA All-Star Game, Bird and the rest of the league embraced him with open arms.

What had started as a rivalry rooted in competition and personal pride blossomed into a bond built on mutual respect and admiration. Bird and Magic had spent years battling each other for supremacy, but through that competition, they developed a deep appreciation for each other's greatness.

The Bird-Magic rivalry might be the most important in sports history—not just for the games they played or the championships they won, but for what it did for the NBA as a whole. They raised the bar for basketball, making the league more exciting and drawing in new fans from all over the world. By pitting the Celtics against the Lakers, East against West, and Bostonians against Angelenos, Bird and Magic turned the NBA into a cultural phenomenon.

More than anything, Bird and Magic proved that even the fiercest competitors can become the closest of friends. Their rivalry was about more than winning and losing—it was about pushing each other to be the best versions of themselves. Their mutual respect serves as a lasting example of what it means to compete at the highest level while still holding your adversary in the highest regard. Bird and Magic's story reminds us that sports are about more than just results; they are about finding common ground through competition and inspiring greatness in one another.

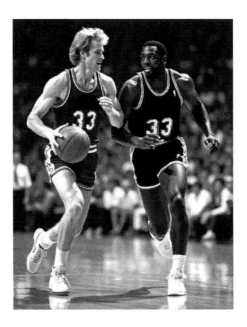

# Fun facts

1) College Rivalry: Bird and Magic first met in the 1979 NCAA Championship, where Magic's Michigan State defeated Bird's Indiana State.

2) MVPs: Between them, Bird and Magic won six NBA MVP awards during the 1980s.

3) Changing the NBA: Their rivalry is credited with reviving the NBA's popularity, turning it into a global phenomenon.

# Trivia

**In which year did Larry Bird and Magic Johnson first face each other in the NBA Finals?**

A) 1984
B) 1985
C) 1986

# CHAPTER 5

## Shaquille O'Neal - Dominance and Charisma

Shaquille O'Neal was simply known as 'Shaq'. He was a dominating force in the NBA like no other. Standing 7 ft 1 in and weighing over 300 lbs, he possessed a lethal combination of size, strength, and athleticism that made him the most unguardable player in the league. The Orlando Magic knew it when they selected the imposing center with the first overall pick in the 1992 draft, and the rest of the NBA would soon learn this same lesson.

Shaq's impact was immediate. In his debut season, he averaged 23.4 points, 13.9 rebounds, and 3.5 blocks per game, earning the title of NBA Rookie of the Year. Fans watched in awe as Shaq dunked over defenders, often shattering backboards. His sheer size alone intimidated his opponents, but he was also an exceptionally skilled athlete who could run the floor, pass, and defend.

Shaq was already impressive, but his real ascension to greatness came in 1996 when he was traded to the Los Angeles Lakers. There, he teamed up with a young Kobe Bryant and led the Lakers to three consecutive NBA titles in 2000, 2001, and 2002. This period marked the absolute prime of Shaq's career. He won three consecutive NBA Finals MVP awards and delivered some of the most dominant Finals performances the game had ever seen. Few, if any, centers could stop him.

Shaq's strength and ability to dominate in the paint led to frequent fouling; opposing teams abandoned attempts to stop him from scoring and instead resorted to fouling him, hoping he'd miss free throws. This strategy was called 'Hack-a-Shaq,' as he struggled with free throws, shooting just 52%. But it didn't work. He was too strong, too skilled, and too determined.

Off the court, Shaq was one of the most popular athletes in sports. He had one of the best senses of humor. He entertained fans with pranks, rapping, starring in movies, and joking in interviews. He was always humble and kind, both on and off the court, taking time to make fans smile and cheer wherever he went. Through his charisma and humility, he became a global superstar, beloved by fans for his magnetic personality.

His personality was as big as his game. Shaq's fame opened up opportunities in various fields, from rap albums to movies like Kazaam, and later, a career as an NBA analyst. Yet, no matter the success and celebrity he achieved as a cultural icon, his love for basketball remained his guiding force. He had no problem playing to the cameras, but when the game was on, it was all business.

Shaquille O'Neal's legacy is one of influence and joy. On the court, he was an unstoppable force, changing the way teams defended with his sheer physicality and leaving a permanent mark on the game. Off the court, he was a fun-loving giant, endearing himself to fans and earning the respect of players. His influence continues to be felt, both as a player and as an ambassador for the game.

Whether through rim-shattering dunks that left his teammates in shock or his endless humor that left audiences laughing, Shaq delivered on every level—both on the court and off—always staying relatable and human. His career serves as an important lesson for all, from today's young fans to the current generation of players: one doesn't always need to dominate to be great, and greatness can be achieved without always being at the top. Next to Wilt Chamberlain, no one was as dominant; next to Michael Jordan, no one reigned so universally. Shaquille O'Neal's ability to combine dominance with joy ensures that he will always be remembered as one of the NBA's greatest stars.

# Fun facts

1) Backboard Breaker: Shaq famously shattered two NBA backboards with powerful dunks during his rookie season.

2) Shaq's Degrees: Despite his fun personality, Shaq is highly educated, holding a doctoral degree in education.

3) Superman: Shaq often referred to himself as "Superman" and even has the famous Superman logo tattooed on his arm.

# Trivia

**How many NBA championships did Shaquille O'Neal win during his career?**

A) 2
B) 3
C) 4

# CHAPTER 6

## Bill Russell - The Champion's Mindset

Bill Russell was perhaps the greatest winner in the history of sports. During his 13-year career in the NBA, he led the Boston Celtics to 11 NBA championships—a record that still stands today. But Russell was more than just a champion; he was a leader, a selfless player, and a fierce competitor.

Russell was born in 1934 in Monroe, Louisiana, a city still gripped by segregation and discrimination. However, he developed a deep love for basketball and quickly made a name for himself as a tenacious defender and rebounder. He played college basketball at the University of San Francisco, where, by his sophomore season, he had led his team to back-to-back NCAA championships in 1955 and 1956. From the very beginning, he was more than just a talented player; he was a natural leader.

Bill Russell's arrival at the Boston Celtics in 1956 immediately transformed the team into a powerhouse. Standing 6 ft 10 in, Russell was a defensive juggernaut, revolutionizing the game with his shot-blocking and rebounding skills. He was an outlier in the league: while many of his contemporaries focused on scoring, Russell prioritized defense, teamwork, and doing whatever was necessary to win. It's no wonder he quickly emerged as a true leader.

While Russell's defensive abilities were legendary, it was his mental approach to the game that set him apart. He hated losing and was fiercely competitive. He treated every game as though no one was working harder than he was, believing he was the secret ingredient to his team's success—even when his contributions didn't show up in the box score. His teammates and, more importantly, his opponents respected him for it.

Russell's defining moments came in the 1960s, when his Celtics faced off against the Los Angeles Lakers in several classic NBA Finals matchups. The Celtics won seven championships during that decade, with Russell's leadership being the key to Boston's success. He was a defensive menace with a knack for making big plays, especially in crucial moments late in games. His reputation as a clutch player grew with each passing year.

In addition to his on-court achievements, Russell broke significant barriers off the court. As the first African American superstar in professional basketball at a time of intense racial tension, Russell overcame both on- and off-court discrimination. In 1966, he became the first African American head coach in any of the four major U.S. professional sports when he was named player-coach of the Celtics, a role in which he won two additional championships.

Bill Russell's legacy extends far beyond his 11 championship rings. He redefined what it means to be a leader, emphasizing the importance of teamwork over individual accolades, and becoming a force of nature fueled by kindness, hard work, and self-sacrifice. He wasn't driven by personal glory or recognition; he was committed to supporting his team, no matter the personal cost. In Russell's view, greatness wasn't about how much he could achieve individually, but how much he could improve the people around him.

# Fun facts

1) First African American Coach: Bill Russell became the first African American head coach in major U.S. professional sports in 1966.

2) Olympic Gold Medalist: Russell won a gold medal with Team USA at the 1956 Olympics before entering the NBA.

3) Defense First: Despite his 11 championships, Russell never averaged more than 19 points per game in a season, focusing instead on defense and rebounding.

# Trivia

**Which team did Bill Russell play for during his entire NBA career?**

A) Los Angeles Lakers
B) Boston Celtics
C) New York Knicks

# CHAPTER 7

## Wilt Chamberlain - The Record Breaker

Wilt Chamberlain was more than just a basketball player; he was a phenomenon. Standing at 7 feet 1 inch tall with skills like no other, Wilt possessed unparalleled athleticism and strength that allowed him to dominate the game in a way that no player ever had before. From his league debut with the Philadelphia Warriors in 1959 until his retirement in 1973, Wilt set records, accomplished the impossible, and cemented his place as one of the greatest basketball players in history.

Perhaps the most impressive achievement of Wilt's career was his ability to score at will. On March 2, 1962, Wilt scored 100 points in a game against the New York Knicks—a feat many believe to be the greatest single-game performance in basketball history. No player has ever come close to this number in any subsequent game. Wilt was unstoppable that night, scoring from all over the court, taking opponents off the dribble for dunks, and even hitting free throws, which were not his strong suit.

His 100-point game was just the beginning. Wilt became the first player to score 30,000 points in his career. He still holds the all-time NBA record for rebounds. During the 1961-62 season, he averaged 50.4 points per game, a record that seems unbreakable. It wasn't just Wilt's size that made him special; it was his combination of size, agility, and stamina. For a man of his height, he could run the floor like a guard, and he routinely played entire games without taking a breather.

Wilt was so dominant that the NBA introduced rule changes to make the game more competitive. Most famously, they widened the lane to make it harder for Wilt to score close to the basket. But it didn't matter—Wilt continued to dominate. No matter the rules, he would find a way to make them work for him.

Wilt Chamberlain was also a great teammate. In his early years, his teams rarely won championships, and critics claimed that while Wilt was a great scorer and rebounder, he wasn't a winner. He heard this criticism and adapted his game, focusing more on passing and defense. In 1967, he led the Philadelphia 76ers to an NBA championship, proving he could win at the highest level. He won another title in 1972 with the Los Angeles Lakers.

Off the court, Wilt was a superstar in every sense. He was one of the first transcendent cultural figures in the NBA. A movie star, author, and volleyball player, Wilt's good looks and magnetic personality made him a global icon and a fan favorite.

Wilt Chamberlain's legacy is one of impossibility and dominance. His records—most notably his 100-point game—remain some of the greatest in sports history. He fundamentally changed the game and influenced generations of players to achieve what they once thought was impossible. The game may have evolved since Wilt's time, but his legacy continues to shape the sport.

Wilt's greatness was the discovery of the limitless potential of the human being. He embodied the idea that nothing is impossible, and that human feats can reach levels we never imagined. With the right combination of genetics, environment, perseverance, and dedication, we, like Wilt, can defy belief. Wilt Chamberlain will always be remembered as the player who expanded the horizons of basketball and took the game into a new realm.

# Fun facts

1) Iron Man: Wilt Chamberlain once played every minute of a season except for 8 minutes, setting a record for minutes played in a season.

2) 50.4 Points Per Game: Wilt averaged 50.4 points per game in the 1961-62 season, a record that still stands today.

3) Volleyball Star: After retiring from basketball, Wilt became a successful volleyball player and was even inducted into the Volleyball Hall of Fame.

# Trivia

**How many points did Wilt Chamberlain score in his record-setting game in 1962?**

A) 100
B) 150
C) 98

# CHAPTER 8

## Stephen Curry - Revolutionizing the Game

Stephen Curry, known for his deadly three-point shooting, has forever changed the game of basketball. When he entered the NBA in 2009, no one could have predicted just how much Curry would revolutionize the sport. At just 6'2" and 185 pounds, Curry didn't have the size or physical dominance of many of his peers. But what he lacked in size, he made up for with skill, work ethic, and a shooting touch that would redefine the game.

Curry's journey began at Davidson College, where his incredible scoring ability put him on the national radar. Despite being doubted by many for his slight frame, Curry's shooting and ball-handling abilities quickly caught the attention of NBA scouts. In 2009, he was drafted by the Golden State Warriors, a decision that would change the future of the franchise and the entire NBA.

What sets Stephen Curry apart is his ability to shoot from virtually anywhere on the court. He is known for his deep three-pointers, often pulling up from well beyond the three-point line, a shot that was once considered too risky. Curry made it look effortless, changing the way teams approached the game. With Curry leading the way, the Warriors built an offense that emphasized spacing, ball movement, and long-range shooting. Soon, other teams around the league began to follow this new model of incredible basketball.

In the 2015-2016 season, Curry set the NBA record for the most three-pointers made in a single season with 402, shattering his own previous record. That same year, he became the first player in NBA history to be unanimously voted the league's Most Valuable Player (MVP). His remarkable ability to hit three-pointers from all angles and distances redefined what was possible on the court, and the era of "positionless" basketball had begun.

Curry's influence extends beyond just his shooting ability. He brought a new level of creativity to the game, combining his shooting with elite ball-handling and passing. His ability to dribble through defenders, find open teammates, or pull up for a quick three-pointer made him nearly impossible to defend. Defenders had to guard Curry the moment he crossed half-court, knowing that he could shoot from anywhere. This spacing opened up opportunities for his teammates, leading to more efficient offenses across the league.

Curry's leadership helped the Golden State Warriors win three NBA championships in 2015, 2017, and 2018. His team set the record for the most wins in a regular season with 73 victories in 2016, breaking a record that had stood for 20 years. Curry's unselfishness, combined with his competitive drive, earned him the respect of his teammates and made the Warriors a dominant force in the league for years.

Beyond his impact on the game itself, Stephen Curry's legacy lies in how he changed the way basketball is played, from the NBA down to the playgrounds. Young players across the world now look up to Curry and try to emulate his deep-range shooting. Coaches, once hesitant to encourage three-point shooting, now emphasize it as a key part of their game plans. Curry showed that a player doesn't have to be the tallest or strongest to dominate the game—skill, preparation, and intelligence can change the sport just as much.

Stephen Curry's revolution of the game will be remembered for generations. He made the impossible seem routine, and in doing so, inspired countless young players to push the limits of what they thought was possible. Curry's ability to innovate and break barriers has made him one of the most influential players in NBA history. His journey shows that with enough dedication and belief in one's abilities, it's possible to change not just a team, but the entire sport.

# Fun facts

1) Unanimous MVP: In 2016, Stephen Curry became the first player in NBA history to win the MVP award by unanimous vote.

2) Family of Athletes: Curry's father, Dell Curry, was also an NBA player, and his younger brother, Seth Curry, is currently an NBA player.

3) Record Breaker: Curry broke the record for most three-pointers in an NBA Finals game by hitting nine threes in Game 2 of the 2018 Finals.

# Trivia

**How many three-pointers did Stephen Curry make during the 2015-2016 NBA season, setting a new record?**

A) 300
B) 350
C) 402

# CHAPTER 9

## Hakeem Olajuwon - Dream Shake

Hakeem Olajuwon, better known as "The Dream," is considered one of the greatest big men in basketball history. Born in Lagos, Nigeria, Olajuwon didn't start playing basketball until the age of 15. Despite starting late, thanks to his natural physicality, work ethic, and desire to improve, he quickly became one of the most dominant players in the game. From a soccer goalkeeper to an NBA champion, his journey exemplifies the power of patience and passion for mastering one's craft.

Hakeem made his college debut by leading the University of Houston to three consecutive Final Four appearances. By the time he made his NBA debut as the No. 1 overall pick in 1984, Olajuwon had already demonstrated glimpses of his immense potential. He was drafted by the Houston Rockets, where he would spend nearly 20 years. Right from the start, it was clear that Hakeem had the ability to excel on both ends of the court.

Hakeem's signature was his remarkable footwork. Unlike other big men of his era, who relied heavily on size and power, Olajuwon combined speed and agility with his 7-foot frame to develop a unique style of play. His signature move, the "Dream Shake," became one of the most dangerous offensive weapons in the NBA. With a series of quick turns, fakes, and spins, Hakeem could easily outmaneuver defenders, leaving them unsure if he would shoot, pass, or drive to the basket.

The Dream Shake wasn't just a flashy move—it was the product of years of dedicated practice. Hakeem honed his footwork tirelessly, benefiting from his soccer background to develop a fluidity rarely seen in centers. His skills were so well-polished that he routinely outplayed opponents much bigger and stronger than himself. Whether posting up on the low block or setting up from the midline, Hakeem was a nightmare to defend.

Beyond his offensive prowess, Olajuwon was one of the best defensive players in NBA history. He still holds the career record for blocks with 3,830 and was a two-time Defensive Player of the Year. Hakeem had an extraordinary ability to read the game—his timing and anticipation allowed him to block shots, disrupt passing lanes, and dominate the paint. Throughout the 1990s, the Houston Rockets were a force to be reckoned with, largely due to his defensive dominance.

Olajuwon's most productive seasons came in 1994 and 1995, when he led the Rockets to back-to-back NBA titles. Both times, he earned NBA Finals MVP honors, showcasing his versatility and leadership. In 1994, he became the first player in NBA history to win the MVP, Defensive Player of the Year, and Finals MVP in the same season. His leadership and determination delivered the Rockets their first-ever championship.

Hakeem Olajuwon's legacy lies in his relentless pursuit of perfection. He wasn't just a player who relied on natural talent—he tirelessly worked to refine his skills, perfect his footwork, and develop one of the most complete games in the history of big men. His influence continues today, as young centers strive to replicate his rare combination of size, finesse, and mobility.

To Olajuwon, the "Dream Shake" was more than just a move—it was his legacy. It embodied his belief that there is no glory without effort, dedication, and a constant drive to improve. Hakeem's career serves as a model for players worldwide, proving that anything is possible if you commit to the journey and remain dedicated to your craft.

# Fun facts

1) Soccer Beginnings: Hakeem Olajuwon played soccer as a goalkeeper before transitioning to basketball, which helped him develop his incredible footwork.

2) Historic Triple Win: In 1994, Hakeem won the NBA MVP, Defensive Player of the Year, and Finals MVP in the same season—an unmatched feat.

3) All-Time Blocks Leader: Hakeem holds the NBA record for most career blocks with 3,830, a mark that still stands today.

# Trivia

**What was Hakeem Olajuwon's signature move called?**

A) The Skyhook
B) The Fadeaway
C) The Dream Shake

# CHAPTER 10

## Dirk Nowitzki - The Loyal Superstar

Changing the world's perception of European basketball is Dirk Nowitzki's lasting legacy. Born in Würzburg, Germany, Nowitzki was far from the typical NBA star, especially compared to those from the U.S. He didn't come from a major U.S. college basketball program, and when he declared for the 1998 NBA Draft, many scouts and observers questioned whether his distinctive European playing style would succeed at the highest level.

Dirk was a shooting savant, known for his silky-smooth stroke, which included his signature one-legged fadeaway—a move that became his trademark. At 7 feet tall, he wasn't a traditional big man. He shot like a guard, including from long range, something that players his size typically didn't do. His ability to space the floor and hit three-pointers made him a nightmare for defenders. Dirk's unique skillset not only changed the game but also redefined the role of the modern power forward. He set the blueprint for what future big men should be able to do from beyond the arc.

Dirk's long-term devotion to the Dallas Mavericks was equally remarkable. He spent 21 seasons as the cornerstone of the organization, playing his entire career for the same franchise —a rare feat in today's NBA. Staying with one team your entire career sends a message: you're committed to that franchise, that city, and its fans. Sure, you could chase rings by moving to other teams, but Dirk wanted to win a ring for the team that drafted him.

That moment came in 2011 when Dirk guided the Mavericks to their first-ever NBA championship. The path to the title was anything but easy. The Mavericks had a reputation for choking in big games, and Dirk had also been labeled as a player who couldn't deliver in the playoffs, especially after the team's infamous Game 7 loss to the Miami Heat in the 2006 NBA Finals. But Dirk never gave up, and his belief in himself and his team paid off when the Mavericks upset the heavily favored Miami Heat in six games, with Dirk earning Finals MVP honors.

Dirk's 2011 championship run is widely regarded as one of the greatest in NBA history. During the Finals, the Mavericks faced the Miami Heat, led by LeBron James, Dwyane Wade, and Chris Bosh—a team that was heavily favored to win. Despite the odds, Dirk delivered clutch performance after clutch performance, making impossible shots in crucial moments. His one-footed fadeaway and calm demeanor under pressure became his trademarks, proving that hard work can overcome any circumstance, regardless of height, age, or background.

That title cemented Dirk's legacy as more than just a great player—it made him a true champion. Dirk didn't chase rings by joining other superstars; he believed in Dallas and in himself, choosing to win on his own terms. His 2011 title was the ultimate vindication of a career built on loyalty, hard work, and faith in his teammates. Dirk's belief in himself and his team paid off in the purest and most rewarding way.

Dirk's influence extended far beyond his on-court play. He opened the door for countless international players, showing them that they could compete with the best and win at the highest level. Dirk was a trailblazer, and today's NBA is filled with international players on championship teams who have followed in his footsteps. He paved the way for the modern power forward—a hybrid player with the skills of a guard, the mindset of a big man, and the shooting range to stretch defenses.

# Fun facts

1) One-Legged Fadeaway: Dirk's signature one-legged fadeaway shot is considered one of the most unguardable moves in NBA history.

2) Most Seasons with One Team: Dirk holds the NBA record for the most seasons played with a single team, with 21 years in Dallas.

3) International Icon: Dirk was the first European player to win the NBA MVP award, earning the honor in 2007.

# Trivia

**How many seasons did Dirk Nowitzki play for the Dallas Mavericks?**

A) 15
B) 21
C) 17

# CHAPTER 11

## Oscar Robertson - The Triple-Double King

Oscar Robertson, known as "The Big O," is one of the most versatile and influential players in the history of basketball. Born in 1938 in Tennessee and raised in Indianapolis, Robertson grew up in a time when African Americans faced significant challenges, both on and off the court. Despite these obstacles, his love for basketball drove him to become one of the most dominant players of his era, forever changing the way the game was played

Robertson entered the NBA in 1960 after an impressive college career at the University of Cincinnati, where he was a three-time College Player of the Year. From the moment he stepped onto an NBA court with the Cincinnati Royals (now the Sacramento Kings), it was clear that Oscar was no ordinary player. At 6'5", he had the size to play multiple positions, and his combination of scoring, rebounding, and passing set him apart from his peers.

What made Oscar Robertson truly special was his ability to record triple-doubles—achieving double digits in points, rebounds, and assists in a single game. During the 1961-1962 season, Robertson made history by becoming the first player in NBA history to average a triple-double for an entire season, with 30.8 points, 12.5 rebounds, and 11.4 assists per game. At the time, this feat was considered unimaginable, and it remained unmatched for over 50 years.

Robertson's dominance wasn't just about filling the stat sheet; it was his basketball IQ and leadership that set him apart. He consistently made the right play at the right time, always putting his team in the best position to win. As a point guard, his vision and passing ability were unmatched, but he could also score at will, driving to the basket with power or pulling up for a mid-range jumper. Defenders found it nearly impossible to stop him, as he could hurt them in so many ways.

Despite his individual success, championships eluded Robertson early in his career. The Royals struggled to build a championship-caliber team around him, and while Oscar continued to post incredible numbers, he couldn't get past the dominant Boston Celtics teams of the 1960s. However, his fortunes changed in 1970 when he was traded to the Milwaukee Bucks, where he teamed up with a young Kareem Abdul-Jabbar.

In 1971, Robertson finally won his first and only NBA championship. The Bucks dominated the playoffs, and Robertson's leadership was key in guiding the team to victory. At 32 years old, the championship was a fitting reward for a player who had spent a decade as one of the best in the game without a title to show for it. His ability to adapt his game and work alongside Kareem proved that he was not just a stat-stuffer, but a true winner.

Oscar Robertson's legacy goes far beyond his statistics. He was a pioneer, both on and off the court. In 1976, his efforts in the landmark Oscar Robertson v. National Basketball Association case led to the introduction of free agency, allowing players more freedom to choose where they played and improving their bargaining power. His fight for player rights reshaped the NBA, giving future generations of players opportunities that he didn't have early in his career.

Today, Robertson is remembered as the original triple-double king, a player whose versatility changed the way basketball was played. His ability to excel in every aspect of the game set a new standard for what was possible on the court. His achievements continue to inspire players like LeBron James and Russell Westbrook, who have followed in his footsteps as do-it-all players. Oscar Robertson will forever be known as a trailblazer, a leader, and one of the greatest to ever play the game.

# Fun facts

1) Triple-Double Pioneer: Oscar Robertson was the first player in NBA history to average a triple-double for an entire season.

2) Free Agency Pioneer: Robertson's legal fight against the NBA in the 1970s led to the introduction of free agency, giving players more rights.

3) NBA Champion: In 1971, Robertson won his first NBA championship with the Milwaukee Bucks, alongside Kareem Abdul-Jabbar.

# Trivia

**In which season did Oscar Robertson average a triple-double for the entire year?**

A) 1960-1961
B) 1961-1962
C) 1963-1964

# CHAPTER 12

## Dr. J and Dunking

Julius "Dr. J" Erving wasn't just a basketball player; he was an artist. With high-flying dunks, smooth transition shots, and extraordinary athleticism, Erving redefined the game. Born in 1950 in Roosevelt, New York, Erving honed his skills on the playground, becoming an avid basketball player who perfected his unique style. Few could have imagined that he would go on to revolutionize the sport and become one of its most influential figures.

Dr. J burst onto the American Basketball Association (ABA) scene, where his above-the-rim dunks and flair for aerial moves captivated fans of all ages. His distinctive afro and unerring style made him one of the most recognizable players on the court. Erving didn't just play basketball; he transformed it into an art form, combining strength with grace effortlessly. He soon became the face of the ABA, winning titles, MVP awards, and establishing himself as one of the league's premier players.

Erving's most iconic moments often came when he was in the air. His ability to take shots mid-air, as though he defied gravity, became legendary. His most famous dunk occurred during the 1976 ABA Slam Dunk Contest, where he soared from the free-throw line to deliver a dunk that left crowds and judges in awe. This dunk, simply known as "The Dunk," became one of the most famous in basketball history, solidifying Dr. J as an early pioneer of above-the-rim play.

When the ABA merged with the NBA in 1976, Dr. J joined the Philadelphia 76ers, where he continued to electrify fans with his aerial displays. Transitioning to the NBA was seamless for Erving, who quickly established himself as one of the league's top players. His ability to captivate audiences with his spectacular dunks and floaters made him a fan favorite, but it was his leadership and consistency that turned the 76ers into perennial contenders.

Dr. J's career culminated with an NBA championship in 1983. He led the 76ers to a four-game victory over the Los Angeles Lakers, securing his long-awaited title. While Erving's individual brilliance was undeniable, the championship proved that he could elevate his teammates and bring a team together. It demonstrated that his game wasn't just about style—it was about substance and winning at the highest level.

Off the court, Dr. J's persona and style made him an influential ambassador for basketball. His charisma helped promote the game both in the U.S. and internationally. Erving didn't just play basketball; he expanded the cultural significance of the sport, blurring the lines between sport and art. For Dr. J, basketball wasn't merely a game—it was a form of creativity and self-expression.

Julius Erving's legacy as "Dr. J" goes beyond highlight-reel plays. He revolutionized basketball and inspired a generation of players to explore new possibilities on the court. His innovation, physical prowess, and ability to overcome challenges redefined the standards of greatness. Without Dr. J, the careers of players like Michael Jordan, Vince Carter, and LeBron James might not have reached the heights they did.

The influence of Dr. J can still be felt in the game today. His ability to merge sport with creativity transformed basketball into a stage where artistic expression became just as essential as skill. The lessons from his career remind us that having fun and embracing the moment can elevate a player from good to legendary. Julius Erving, as a pioneer, a champion, and the original high-flyer, will forever be remembered for taking basketball to new heights—both literally and metaphorically.

# Fun facts

1) The Dunk: Dr. J's free-throw line dunk in the 1976 Slam Dunk Contest is one of the most famous plays in basketball history.

2) ABA to NBA Legend: Dr. J won championships in both the ABA and the NBA, becoming one of the few players to dominate both leagues.

3) Influencing Future Generations: Erving's style of play heavily influenced legends like Michael Jordan, who cited Dr. J as one of his biggest inspirations.

# Trivia

**From where did Julius Erving take off to complete his famous dunk in the 1976 Slam Dunk Contest?**

A) The three-point line
B) The free-throw line
C) The half-court line

# CHAPTER 13

## Scottie Pippen - The Ultimate Teammate

Scottie Pippen is often regarded as the ultimate teammate, a player who did all the little things that helped turn a good team into a championship team. While Michael Jordan was the face of the Chicago Bulls, Pippen was the heart of the team, playing a crucial role in their six NBA championships. Pippen was known for his versatility, defensive prowess, and unselfishness, making him one of the best all-around players in NBA history.

Born in Hamburg, Arkansas, Pippen didn't have the traditional path to stardom. He wasn't highly recruited out of high school, but his hard work and determination eventually earned him a scholarship at the University of Central Arkansas. Even then, few could have predicted the impact he would have on the NBA. Pippen's rise to greatness was fueled by his relentless work ethic and his desire to improve every aspect of his game. When the Chicago Bulls traded for Pippen on draft night in 1987, they had no idea that they were getting one of the most complete players the league would ever see.

Pippen's versatility was his greatest strength. At 6'8", he could play almost every position on the court, and his combination of size, athleticism, and basketball IQ made him a nightmare for opponents. Pippen was an elite defender, capable of guarding the opposing team's best player, whether that was a guard, forward, or even a center. He was named to the NBA All-Defensive First Team eight times during his career, earning a reputation as one of the best defenders the game has ever seen.

On offense, Pippen was just as valuable. While Jordan often took the spotlight as the primary scorer, Pippen was the glue that held everything together. He could score when needed, but he excelled as a playmaker, distributing the ball and making sure his teammates were involved. His court vision and basketball intelligence allowed him to run the Bulls' offense efficiently, taking pressure off Jordan and allowing the team to thrive as a unit.

The defining moment of Pippen's career came during the Chicago Bulls' two three-peat runs in the 1990s. From 1991 to 1993 and again from 1996 to 1998, Pippen and Jordan led the Bulls to six NBA championships, solidifying their place as one of the greatest duos in sports history. Pippen's willingness to take on the tough assignments, both offensively and defensively, allowed Jordan to flourish, but his contributions went far beyond just being a sidekick. Pippen's all-around play, leadership, and ability to step up in crucial moments were key to the Bulls' dynasty.

When Jordan briefly retired in 1993, Pippen took on the role of the team's leader. During the 1993-1994 season, he led the Bulls to a 55-win season and was named the NBA All-Star Game MVP. This season showcased Pippen's ability to carry a team on his own, proving that he was more than just a second option. His leadership and humility, even in Jordan's absence, earned him respect across the league.

Pippen's legacy is not just about the championships or the individual accolades—it's about how he approached the game. He was always willing to sacrifice his own stats for the good of the team, putting winning above personal glory. His defensive intensity, basketball intelligence, and team-first mentality set a standard for what it means to be a great teammate. Pippen redefined the role of the "supporting star," showing that being unselfish and doing the little things can lead to greatness.

Today, Scottie Pippen is remembered as one of the most complete players in NBA history. His ability to impact the game in every way—scoring, passing, defending, and leading—made him a vital part of one of the greatest dynasties the NBA has ever seen. His journey from a small-town player to an NBA legend is a testament to hard work, dedication, and the belief that individual success is always secondary to the team's success.

# Fun facts

1) Versatility King: Pippen is one of the few players in NBA history to record more than 15,000 points, 6,000 assists, and 2,000 steals in his career.

2) First in Olympic History: Pippen, along with Michael Jordan, was part of the first-ever Olympic "Dream Team" that won the gold medal in 1992.

3) Defensive Master: Pippen was named to the NBA All-Defensive First Team eight times, making him one of the best defenders in NBA history.

# Trivia

**How many NBA championships did Scottie Pippen win with the Chicago Bulls?**

A) 6
B) 5
C) 7

# CHAPTER 14
## Allen Iverson - The Answer

Allen Iverson, known as "The Answer," redefined toughness on the basketball court. Despite being only 6 feet tall and weighing 165 lbs, Iverson played with the heart of a giant, fearlessly driving to the rim against much larger opponents. Growing up in the suburbs of Hampton, Virginia, Iverson faced numerous hardships, but basketball and football gave him the inspiration to rise above them. By the time he reached the NBA, Iverson had already built a reputation as one of the most exciting and fearless players to ever lace up a pair of sneakers.

Iverson was drafted number one overall by the Philadelphia 76ers in 1996, and within weeks, he proved that size didn't define him. With his incredible speed, crossover dribble, and finishing ability at the rim, he was almost impossible to defend. Iverson won NBA Rookie of the Year in his debut season, but it wasn't just about the award. He was best known for his "killer crossover," a move that became one of the most famous in NBA history and even embarrassed players like Michael Jordan.

Iverson's greatest strength wasn't just his skills, but his tenacity and character. Coming from a poverty-stricken family and facing legal troubles before his NBA career, Iverson knew how to persevere. This fighting spirit was evident every time he stepped onto the court. Despite taking hard fouls from bigger players, Iverson never backed down. He was a warrior in every sense, playing through pain and carrying the Sixers on his back night after night.

Iverson's best season came in 2000-2001, when he led the 76ers to the NBA Finals. That year, he earned the NBA MVP award, averaging 31.1 points per game—making him one of the smallest players ever to win the league's most coveted individual honor. In Game 1 of the Finals against the heavily favored Los Angeles Lakers, Iverson scored 48 points to lead the Sixers to an upset victory, famously stepping over Lakers guard Tyronn Lue after making a decisive basket. Although the Sixers ultimately lost the series, Iverson's grit and determination became legendary.

Iverson's impact extended beyond points and awards—he changed the culture of the NBA. With his cornrows, tattoos, and unapologetic attitude, Iverson brought hip-hop culture into the mainstream of basketball. He played with a swagger and flair that resonated with fans all over the world, especially the younger generation. Iverson was more than just a basketball player; he was a cultural icon. His influence reached beyond the court, encouraging young players to be authentic and true to themselves both on and off the hardwood.

However, Iverson's career wasn't without controversy. His refusal to conform—most famously encapsulated by his now-iconic "I don't need to practice" rant—led to friction with coaches and management. Yet, even in the face of scandals, Iverson remained true to himself, earning respect for his authenticity. As the league evolved and new superstars emerged, Iverson's legacy endured. Fans continued to admire his aggressive play and relentless determination to defy the odds.

Allen Iverson is a man that does more than just play basketball, he is a man of perseverance, character and self-belief. Though never a NBA champion, Iverson was considered one of the greatest players of all time. With his love, his determination and not giving up, he was an inspiration in the sport. He demonstrated that you don't have to be a small guy to be able to battle the game giants with enough guts and belief.

Many will remember Iverson as "The Answer" — the player who proved that it is all heart, passion and the will to fight through the battles. He continues to be a part of the NBA today, as players continue to invent on and off the court. Iverson's life tale is one of resilience in the face of tragedy, and that inspires a generation to believe in themselves, to never fail an experiment.

# Fun facts

1) Crossover Master: Iverson's "killer crossover" is one of the most famous moves in NBA history, even catching Michael Jordan off guard.

2) Rookie of the Year: Iverson was named NBA Rookie of the Year in 1997 after averaging 23.5 points per game in his debut season.

3) Cultural Icon: Iverson brought hip-hop culture into the NBA, influencing the league's fashion and attitude, making him a symbol of authenticity and individuality.

# Trivia

**How many points did Allen Iverson score in Game 1 of the 2001 NBA Finals against Los Angeles Lakers?**

A) 48

B) 25

C) 53

# CHAPTER 15

## Nikola Jokić - The Versatile Big Man

Nikola Jokić, often referred to as "The Joker," has redefined what it means to be a big man in the modern NBA. Born in Sombor, Serbia, Jokić wasn't expected to become one of the best players in the league when he was drafted by the Denver Nuggets in 2014 as the 41st overall pick. In fact, few people knew his name, and fewer expected him to become an NBA superstar. Yet, through hard work, basketball intelligence, and a unique skill set for a player of his size, Jokić has emerged as one of the most dominant and versatile players in the world.

At 7 feet tall and weighing over 250 pounds, Jokić moves with an elegance and finesse that seems almost impossible for someone of his stature. But what sets him apart from other centers is his passing ability. Jokić is often compared to a point guard, thanks to his incredible court vision and knack for threading passes through defenses with pinpoint accuracy. From no-look passes to behind-the-back assists, Jokić's creativity with the basketball has redefined the center position, showing that big men can do far more than just score in the paint or protect the rim.

Jokić's rise to stardom wasn't immediate. When he first arrived in Denver, he was seen as a skilled but slow player, overshadowed by other prospects. However, his basketball IQ and unselfishness quickly earned him a starting spot with the Nuggets. Jokić's ability to control the game from the center position, dictating the offense and setting up his teammates, made him the focal point of Denver's strategy. It wasn't long before the league took notice.

By the 2020-2021 season, Jokić had cemented himself as the best passing big man in NBA history and one of the most impactful players in the league. That year, he became the first center since Shaquille O'Neal to win the NBA MVP award, averaging 26.4 points, 10.8 rebounds, and 8.3 assists per game. His MVP campaign highlighted not only his individual excellence but also his ability to make everyone around him better. Jokić wasn't just scoring points—he was orchestrating the offense, setting the tempo, and making his teammates shine.

What makes Jokić's game so unique is his ability to adapt and find ways to contribute in every aspect of the game. Whether it's grabbing a rebound, setting a perfect screen, or hitting a clutch shot, Jokić is always involved. His leadership on the court is calm but commanding, as he often controls the flow of the game without needing to be flashy. His skill set is a perfect blend of old-school fundamentals and modern-day versatility, allowing him to dominate in ways that defy traditional expectations for a big man.

Jokić's shooting touch is another key element of his game. He has a soft touch from mid-range and can hit three-pointers with consistency, making him a threat from anywhere on the court. His ability to space the floor and create plays off the dribble allows the Nuggets to run an offense that is incredibly difficult to defend. Jokić has shown that today's centers must be multifaceted, capable of scoring, passing, and shooting, all while maintaining a high level of basketball IQ.

Beyond his individual accolades, Jokić's ultimate goal is team success. Under his leadership, the Denver Nuggets have become a perennial playoff contender, and his unselfish style of play has been key to their rise. While his MVPs and individual stats are impressive, Jokić is always quick to credit his teammates, embodying the spirit of a true team player.

Jokić's journey from a second-round draft pick to a two-time NBA MVP (2021, 2022) is a testament to the power of skill, perseverance, and vision. He has shown that you don't need to be the most athletic or the most flashy player to dominate the game—you just need to understand the game better than anyone else. Nikola Jokić is not only redefining what it means to be a great center, but he is also paving the way for future generations of big men to expand their games and embrace new roles on the court.

# Fun facts

1) Second-Round Steal: Jokić was drafted 41st overall in 2014, making him the lowest-drafted player ever to win the NBA MVP award.

2) Triple-Double Machine: Jokić regularly records triple-doubles, thanks to his ability to contribute in points, rebounds, and assists from the center position.

3)Sombor Shuffle: Jokić's signature shot, the "Sombor Shuffle," is a one-legged fadeaway that he developed as a response to an ankle injury, and it's nearly impossible to defend.

# Trivia

**In which year did Nikola Jokić win his first NBA MVP award?**

A) 2018
B) 2022
C) 2021/C

# CHAPTER 16
## The Dream Team - A Golden Legacy

In 1992, the United States sent what is arguably the greatest basketball team ever assembled to the Barcelona Olympics. Known as The Dream Team, it featured 11 NBA legends and one college player, forming an unstoppable force. The roster included names like Michael Jordan, Magic Johnson, Larry Bird, Charles Barkley, and Scottie Pippen, among others. This was the first time NBA players were allowed to compete in the Olympics, and the result left the world in awe.

The Dream Team wasn't just a squad of NBA superstars — it symbolized the global reach and power of the NBA. After years of U.S. amateur teams failing to secure gold, The Dream Team was created with one clear mission: to restore American dominance in basketball. But they didn't just win; they demolished the competition, winning each game by an average of 44 points. Their flashy performances made them international celebrities and inspired millions of people worldwide to pick up a basketball for the first time.

From the start, The Dream Team was a powerhouse. They won their opening game against Angola with a score of 116-48, setting the tone for the tournament. Jordan's scoring, Magic Johnson's leadership, and Barkley's toughness were all vital components of the team's success, but what truly made The Dream Team special was how these superstars set aside their egos to work together. Despite their varied styles and massive reputations, they played with great heart and cohesion.

Each game was a display of basketball excellence, with memorable moments that still resonate today. Larry Bird's sharp shooting, Karl Malone's dominance in the post, and David Robinson's defensive prowess left their opponents stunned. Even though the opposing teams knew they were likely to lose, they were often thrilled just to share the court with their basketball idols. Players from opposing teams eagerly asked for autographs and photos, further demonstrating The Dream Team's global appeal. They weren't just competitors — they were legends.

The Dream Team's dominance culminated in a gold medal win against Croatia, with a final score of 117-85. Yet their impact extended far beyond the medal podium. The team's presence at the Olympics transformed basketball into a truly international sport. Their performances sparked a global movement, with young athletes around the world aspiring to emulate Michael Jordan's scoring, Magic Johnson's playmaking, or Larry Bird's shooting. The NBA's popularity exploded internationally, and basketball schools flourished across the globe.

One of the lasting legacies of The Dream Team is the emergence of international basketball superstars in the following years. Players like Dirk Nowitzki, Manu Ginóbili, and later Luka Dončić grew up watching The Dream Team and were inspired to pursue their own NBA careers. The Dream Team didn't just dominate the court; they ushered in a new era where the best basketball players weren't only from the U.S., but from all over the world.

The Dream Team remains the gold standard for basketball excellence. They showed the world what could be achieved when the best players unite with a common goal. Their influence is still felt today, as NBA teams and players worldwide strive to reach the level of greatness The Dream Team exemplified in 1992.

The Dream Team revolutionized basketball, turning it into a global phenomenon and inspiring countless players to dream big. They weren't just Olympians — they were cultural icons whose influence extended beyond the game. The Dream Team will always be remembered as the greatest basketball team ever assembled and the group that transformed basketball into a true international sport.

# Fun facts

1) First NBA Players: The 1992 Dream Team was the first Olympic team to feature NBA players, which was allowed after a rule change in 1989.

2) Magic and Bird Together: Although Magic Johnson and Larry Bird had been rivals in the NBA for years, they teamed up on the Dream Team, creating one of the most iconic pairings in basketball history.

3) Cultural Phenomenon: The Dream Team's impact extended beyond sports—they were featured in commercials, magazines, and even had their own line of merchandise, becoming cultural icons.

# Trivia

**In which city did the Dream Team win the Olympic gold medal in 1992?**

A) Paris
B) Barcelona
C) Madrid

# CHAPTER 17
## Dwyane Wade - Flash and Heart

Dwyane Wade (aka "Flash" because of his fast feet and ball movement) is one of the best shooting guards in NBA history. In Chicago, Illinois, Wade surrounded himself with basketball greats such as Michael Jordan. He did not have an easy road to the NBA but he overcame each obstacle with focus, hard work and a passion for the game. By the time he was taken in 2003 by the Miami Heat, as the fifth overall pick, Wade was already in the works.

Wade had an impressive rookie season, but it wasn't until the 2005-06 season that he truly became one of the league's elite players. That year, Wade led the Miami Heat to their first-ever NBA championship, earning NBA Finals MVP honors at the age of 24. His performance in Game 3 of the Finals, where he scored 42 points and led the Heat to a dramatic comeback victory over the Dallas Mavericks, became legendary. Wade's ability to rise in clutch moments earned him the nickname "Flash," as he seemed to accelerate and take control of games when it mattered most.

Wade was known for his explosive scoring, defensive prowess, and ability to block shots — an impressive feat for a 6'4" player. He was one of the quickest, most athletic finishers at the rim, often absorbing contact and still managing to sink difficult shots. But Wade wasn't just a scorer; he was a leader on and off the court, driven by hustle, heart, and determination.

If Wade's 2006 championship cemented his stardom, his legacy only grew from there. In 2010, Wade brought LeBron James and Chris Bosh to Miami, forming the "Big Three." Together, they led the Heat to four consecutive NBA Finals appearances, winning titles in 2012 and 2013. While LeBron often dominated, it was Wade's grit and ruthlessness that made the difference for Miami. He had already proven he could win on his own, but sharing the stage with other superstars showed his maturity and unwavering commitment to winning.

Wade's influence extended beyond the court. He became a role model for young players and an ambassador for basketball. Off the court, he was deeply involved in charitable work, supporting vulnerable children and families. Wade's journey from the streets of Chicago to NBA stardom inspired countless people, and his impact was felt not just in Miami but also in his hometown.

During his farewell "One Last Dance" tour in 2019, Wade was celebrated by fans across the league. His final season was a tribute to all that he had given to the game — his heart, passion, and ability to rise to the occasion. Wade capped his career by posting a triple-double in his final home game for the Miami Heat, a fitting conclusion to an excellence-filled journey.

Dwyane Wade left a legacy of intensity, resilience, and compassion. Despite suffering numerous injuries throughout his career, Wade always bounced back, proving that success is not just about talent — it's about the will to win. With three NBA championships, a Finals MVP award, and numerous All-Star appearances, Wade solidified his place among the greatest players of all time. He masterfully balanced individual greatness with team success, making him one of the most revered figures in basketball.

Wade's legend continues to inspire, not just for his highlight-reel moments, but for his contributions to the sport and his community. He thrilled fans, inspired future generations, and left a lasting impact on the game. Whether it was hitting the game-winning shot, leading his team in the biggest moments, or giving back to those around him, Wade's legacy will endure for years to come.

# Fun facts

1) MVP in 2006 Finals: Wade was named NBA Finals MVP in 2006 for leading the Miami Heat to their first championship.

2) Big Three: Wade, LeBron James, and Chris Bosh formed the "Big Three," leading the Miami Heat to consecutive championships in 2012 and 2013.

3) Shot Blocker: Despite being a guard, Wade is one of the most prolific shot blockers in NBA history, recording over 800 blocks during his career.

# Trivia

**Which team did Dwyane Wade play against in the 2006 NBA Finals when he won his first Finals MVP?**

A) Bulls
B) Celtics
C) Maverick

# CHAPTER 18
## Giannis Antetokounmpo - The Greek Freak

One of the most incredible NBA stories is the rise of Giannis Antetokounmpo to superstardom. Born in Athens, Greece, to Nigerian immigrants, Giannis grew up in poverty, often selling items on the streets to help support his family. Basketball became his refuge, and ultimately the game that would change his life. Scouts recognized his work ethic, speed, and athleticism, leading the Milwaukee Bucks to draft him 15th overall in the 2013 NBA Draft.

When Giannis entered the NBA, he was a lanky 6'9" point guard with plenty of potential but little experience in top-tier leagues. However, his commitment to improvement and relentless work ethic soon became evident. Over the next few years, Giannis reshaped his body, refined his skills, and evolved into one of the most unstoppable players in NBA history. His unique combination of size, speed, and agility earned him the nickname "The Greek Freak" because he was able to perform on the court in ways players his size typically couldn't.

Giannis's rise to NBA stardom took time, but nothing could stop his progress. As he matured, he became a more versatile player, capable of playing all five positions. He could handle the ball, score in the paint, defend multiple positions, and even lead fast breaks. His well-rounded game, combined with his passion for winning, made him the centerpiece of the Milwaukee Bucks' rebuilding efforts.

In 2019, Giannis won his first NBA MVP award, solidifying his place as one of the league's best players. His stats were remarkable, averaging nearly 28 points, 12 rebounds, and 6 assists per game, but what set him apart was his leadership and drive. Giannis wasn't just focused on his own success—he wanted to bring a championship back to Milwaukee, a city that hadn't won an NBA title in decades. He followed up with another MVP award in 2020, dominating both ends of the floor and leading the Bucks to the top of the Eastern Conference.

The crowning achievement of Giannis's career came in 2021 when he led the Milwaukee Bucks to their first NBA championship in 50 years. The Bucks faced the Phoenix Suns in the Finals, and Giannis delivered one of the greatest performances in NBA Finals history. In Game 6, with the Bucks trailing in the series, Giannis erupted for 50 points, 14 rebounds, and 5 blocks, leading Milwaukee to a 105-98 victory and securing the championship. For his heroic efforts, Giannis was named Finals MVP.

Giannis's journey to this title was marked by years of sacrifice and hard work. He transformed from a raw, unpolished player into one of the most complete and dominant forces in the NBA. However, what truly defined Giannis's legacy was not just his basketball achievements, but his humility, work ethic, and dedication to his teammates. Despite all his individual success, Giannis consistently credited his family, coaches, and teammates for helping him reach the top. His rise to basketball stardom serves as an inspiration to millions worldwide.

Giannis Antetokounmpo's story is still being written, but he is already one of the most successful players of his generation. His perseverance, humility, and character have made him a role model for young athletes, while his all-around game has redefined what it means to be a modern NBA player. Giannis's decision to stay with the small-market Milwaukee Bucks, signing a long-term contract extension in 2020 despite lucrative offers from bigger teams, further solidified his status as a beloved figure in the basketball world.

Beyond basketball, Giannis's life is a story of redemption and resilience. He has shown that with discipline, hard work, and the right mindset, anything is possible. From selling trinkets on the streets of Greece to hoisting the Larry O'Brien Trophy as an NBA champion, Giannis's journey serves as a beacon of hope for anyone striving for greatness, no matter their background.

# Fun facts

1) 50-Point Game: Giannis scored 50 points in Game 6 of the 2021 NBA Finals, securing the Bucks' first championship in 50 years.

2) Two-Time MVP: Giannis won back-to-back NBA MVP awards in 2019 and 2020.

3) Family Legacy: Giannis is one of four brothers who have played professional basketball, with two of his brothers, Thanasis and Kostas, also winning NBA championships.

# Trivia

**In which year did Giannis Antetokounmpo win his first NBA championship with the Milwaukee Bucks?**

A) 2021
B) 2020
C) 2019

# Thank you for reading!

As you turn the final page of "Unbelievable Basketball Stories," you've journeyed through the lives and legends that shaped the game we love. These stories of courage, determination, and unforgettable moments on the field remind us that basketball is more than just a sport—it's a reflection of the human spirit. The legends you've read about overcame obstacles, broke barriers, and inspired generations. Let their stories inspire you to dream big, work hard, and never give up, both on and off the field. The game of basketball is full of endless possibilities, and your story might just be the next one to be told.

# TRIVIA SOLUTIONS

**How many NBA championhips did Michael Jordan win with the Bulls?**
(Chapter 1-pag 7)

c) 6

**Against with team did Kobe Bryant score his 81 points**
(Chapter 2- pag 13)

b) Toronto Raptors

**How many NBA championships has Lebron James won?**
(Chapter 3- pag 20)

c) 4

**In which year did Larry Bird and Magic Johnson first face each other in the NBA Finals?**
(Chapter 4- pag 27)

a) 1984

**How many NBA championships did Shaquille O'Neal win during his career?**
(Chapter 5- pag 34)

c) 4

**Which team did Bill Russel play during his entire NBA career?**
(Chapter 6- pag 40 )

b) Boston Celtics

**How many points did Wilt Chamberlain score in his record-setting game in 1962?**
(Chapter 7- pag 46)

a) 100

**How many three-pointers did Stephen Curry make during the 2015-2016 NBA season, setting a new record?**
(Chapter 8- pag 53)

c) 42

**What was Hakeem Olajuwon's signature move called?**
(Chapter 9- pag 59)

c) The dream shake

**How many seasons did Dirk Nowitzki play for the Dallas Maverick?**
(Chapter 10- pag 65)

b) 21

**In which season did Oscar Robertson average a triple-double for the entire year?**
(Chapter 11- pag 71)

b) 1961-1964

**From where did Julius Erving take off to complete his famous dunk in the 1976 Slam Dunk Contest?**
(Chapter 12- pag 77)

b) The free-throw line

How many NBA championships did Scottie Pippen win with the Chicago Bulls?

(Chapter 13- pag 84)

a) 6

How many points did Allen Iverson score in Game 1 of the 2011 NBA Finals against Los Angeles Lakers?

(Chapter 14- pag 90)

a) 48

In wich year did Nikola Jokic win his first NBA MVP award?

(Chapter 15- pag 96)

c) 2021

In which city did the Dream Team win the Olympic gold medal in 1992?

(Chapter 16- pag 102)

b) Barcelona

Which team did Dwyane Wade play against in the 2006 NBA Finals when he won his first Finals MVP?

(Chapter 17 - pag 108)

c) Maverick

How many innings did the longest game in professional baseball history last?

(Chapter 18- pag 114)

a) 2021

# SPECIAL BONUS

## Want this bonus book for FREE?

Get **FREE** unlimited access to it and all of our new books by joining our community!

Published by:

Dream Bigger Books

IMAGINE. EXPLORE.

Made in United States
Troutdale, OR
12/10/2024

26262455R00071